Nothosaurus

Written by Rupert Oliver
Illustrated by Roger Payne

Library of Congress Cataloging in Publication Data

Oliver, Rupert.
  Nothosaurus.

  Summary: Describes the physical characteristics, habits, and natural environment of the dinosaur known as Nothosaurus.
  1. Nothosaurus—Juvenile literature.   [1. Nothosaurus.
2. Dinosaurs]   I. Payne, Roger, fl. 1969-   ill.
II. Title.
QE862.NrO45   1984   567.9'3   84-17796
  ISBN 0-86592-208-X

Rourke Enterprises, Inc.
Vero Beach, FL 32964

Rhamphorhynchus

Pteranodon

Pterodactyl

Ankylosaurus

Dimetrodon

Iguanodon

Tricondon

Nothosaurus

Archaeopteryx

Ichthyosaurus

Plesiosaurus

Deinonychus

Nothosaurus

The storm was over. For days the wind had blown with tremendous fury and the huge waves had smashed themselves against the rocks, throwing spray into the air. Everything was quiet again now.

Nothosaurus had been frightened by the fury of the storm. She had taken shelter inland where the waves could not reach her. Now that the wind and waves had gone, Nothosaurus returned to the beach to look for food. She was very hungry, but she would be able to catch some fish out at sea. Carefully, Nothosaurus picked her way across the beach. The shoreline was scattered with the debris thrown up by the storm.

Using her powerful legs and strong tail, Nothosaurus swam out to sea. Nothosaurus was a strong swimmer, but something was wrong today. She could not swim as fast as usual. Inside her body Nothosaurus was carrying eggs. They were almost ready to be laid. It was the extra weight of the eggs that was slowing Nothosaurus down. Soon she would go ashore to lay her eggs, but now she was hungry.

In the air a pair of Rhamphorhyncus swooped and wheeled. Like Nothosaurus, the Rhamphorhyncus were hunting for fish. They could swoop down out of the sky and snap the fish up in their jaws. Nothosaurus noticed they were circling over one particular place. Slowly Nothosaurus swam over to where the Rhamphorhyncus were circling.

As Nothosaurus drew near to the Rhamphorhyncus she could see a school of fish beneath the surface of the sea. Slowly, so as not to frighten the fish, Nothosaurus swam nearer the fish. She judged the distance between herself and the fish and when she was in the right position, Nothosaurus dashed forward, but she had forgotten that she could not move as fast as usual. Before Nothosaurus could reach the school of fish, a swift Mixosaurus had appeared. The Mixosaurus dashed in among the school. It snapped up fish in its sharp teeth and then swam on.

By the time Nothosaurus had reached the position of the school the fish had scattered in alarm. Nothosaurus was still hungry but no matter how hard she tried, she was too slow to catch any fish. Perhaps the storm had washed some food up on to the beach.

Wearily, Nothosaurus swam back to the beach. She was feeling very hungry as she dragged herself out of the water. A sudden movement startled her. Another creature was on the beach.

Nothosaurus looked around carefully. The other creature might be a fierce hunter that would want to make a meal out of Nothosaurus. The creature was a Placodus.

Nothosaurus had nothing to fear. The Placodus and its companion walked past Nothosaurus and into the sea. There they splashed about looking for shellfish on which to feed. Relieved that she was in no danger, Nothosaurus walked along the beach. She was looking for food.

Along the shoreline Nothosaurus found quite a lot of food. The storm had washed many shell fish on to the beach. As Nothosaurus moved along the beach she passed another large reptile. The Tanystropheus was using its long neck to catch fish. It took no notice of Nothosaurus as she wandered past.

Having eaten enough food to last her for some time, Nothosaurus lay down to rest. She could not settle down. Something was troubling Nothosaurus. It was time for her to lay her eggs. Nothosaurus climbed to her feet and carried on walking.

Nothosaurus was looking for a place to lay her eggs. She knew that if she laid them out in the open, the eggs would soon be eaten by other creatures. She would have to hide them somewhere.

Before long, Nothosaurus came to the entrance to a cave. The cave would make a very good place to hide her eggs. The cave was close to the sea so that when the young Nothosaurus hatched out they would not have far to travel to reach the water. Few creatures lived in caves, so the eggs would not be found easily.

As Nothosaurus scrambled over the beach to reach the cave mouth she was startled by something passing over her head. The creature that glided past was a Kuehneosaur. Nothosaurus seldom saw a Kuehneosaur down on the beach. Kuehneosaurs preferred to live inland among the trees.

Nothosaurus walked into the cave.

The cave was damp and dark. As she entered the cave, Nothosaurus sniffed the air. There were no scents of other animals. Her eggs would be safe. As she peered into the dark, Nothosaurus could see that the cave was quite large and that moss grew on the walls.

Nothosaurus walked into the cave, slipping on some of the wet stones. Further in, the floor of the cave was dry and the air not so damp. This would be a good place to lay her eggs, thought Nothosaurus.

Using her forefeet Nothosaurus dug a shallow hole. When she was satisfied with the hole Nothosaurus stopped digging. Then she squatted over the hole and began to lay her eggs. It took some time, but finally she had laid all her eggs.

Nothosaurus began to cover the eggs with loose stones and sand. No sooner had she begun to do this than Nothosaurus heard a strange sound. Creaks and groans echoed around the dark cave. Then a stone crashed to the ground near to Nothosaurus. Looking up she saw a whole section of the cave roof give way and fall. The cave was collapsing.

The storm which had hit the shore had also weakened the cave walls. Once the first stone fell, it started a collapse. The rest of the cave was now falling in.

Nothosaurus stopped trying to cover the eggs. She ran for the cave mouth in a panic. All about her, boulders and rocks were smashing to the ground. If she did not escape soon, she would be buried alive beneath the stones. Nothosaurus raced for the daylight. A rock hit her a glancing blow but still she ran.

Gasping for breath Nothosaurus dashed out into the sunlight. Moments later the whole cave collapsed with a tremendous roar. Nothosaurus escaped. As soon as Nothosaurus realized that she was safe she lay down to rest. While she was lying exhausted a small furry Morganucodon scampered on to a rock.

Nothosaurus raised her head. The beach was peaceful and she was hungry. She would swim faster now. Nothosaurus splashed into the sea in search of fish.

Nothosaurus and Triassic Europe

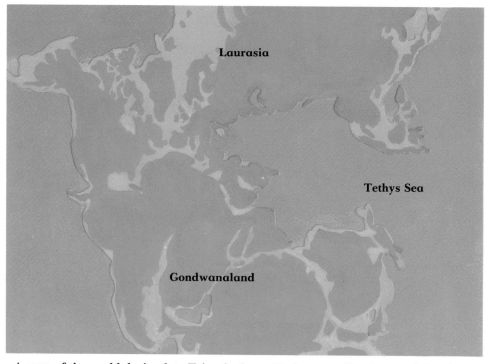

A map of the world during late Triassic times. Nothosaurus lived around the shores of the Tethys Sea. The outlines of modern continents are shown in dark brown.

When did Nothosaurus live?

Nothosaurus roamed the seashore about 210 million years ago. It lived during the Triassic period which lasted from 225 million years ago until 193 million years ago. The Triassic was the first period in the Age of the Dinosaurs, which is known as the Mesozoic Era. The other two periods in the Mesozoic were the Jurassic and the Cretaceous. The Mesozoic Era ended 65 million years ago.

Where did Nothosaurus live?

In the days of the Nothosaurus the continents of the world were very different from those of today. For instance, north-east Africa and India were not then joined to Asia. Instead, there was a large ocean which stretched from Spain right across to Australia and south-east Asia. Scientists have named this ancient ocean Tethys.

It was on the shores of Tethys that the Nothosaurus lived and hunted. In the middle of the Tethys, where Poland is today, was a large island which scientists have called the Isle of Gliny. The rocks of this island have produced some very important fossils. From these fossils scientists have learned much about the animals that lived there. It is on the rocky shores of the Isle of Gliny that our story is set.

What did Nothosaurus eat?

Because there are no Nothosaurs alive today, we cannot say for certain what they ate. Scientists have to collect fossil evidence and then decide what these large reptiles were most likely to have eaten when they were alive.

We know that Nothosaurus lived on the seashore so it must have found its food there. By studying the bones of Nothosaurs, scientists have found that they were very good swimmers and probably spent much of the time in the sea. A hunter will spend most of its time where there is plenty of food. Therefore Nothosaurus must have found most of its food actually in the sea. The fossilized teeth of Nothosaurus are sharp and pointed. These would have made the animal's jaws into a fish-trap. Nothosaurus ate fish.

Young Nothosaurs

Nothosaurus was a reptile and this meant that it laid eggs. Reptiles cannot lay eggs in the water so Nothosaurus had to come ashore to lay its eggs. It is thought that the mother Nothosaurus would abandon her eggs soon after she laid them. The young Nothosaurs would have to look after themselves. Many fossils of young Nothosaurs have been found in what were once caves. Perhaps caves were safe places to hide. As soon as a young Nothosaur was old enough it would leave the beach and head out to sea.

The Nothosaurus Family Tree

Nothosaurus was a reptile which lived about 210 million years ago. It must therefore have evolved from earlier reptiles. These reptiles probably lived on the land and were not very good swimmers. Unfortunately no one has found fossils of a reptile that could possibly be the ancestor of Nothosaurus. Therefore, we do not know how Nothosaurus evolved nor to which reptiles it is related. Scientists are almost certain that they know how Nothosaurus evolved.

Soon after Nothosaurus disappeared a new group of marine reptiles appeared; the Plesiosaurs. By studying their fossils, scientists have shown that the Plesiosaurs could have descended from Nothosaurus. The Plesiosaurus's neck was slightly longer than that of the Nothosaurus, and its head slightly smaller. Instead of the sturdy legs of the Nothosaurus, the Plesiosaurs had strong flippers, which were much better for swimming. Apart from these differences the skeletons of the Plesiosaurs were very like those of the Nothosaurs. This is why scientists think that they may be related.

Other Triassic Reptiles

In our story, Nothosaurus encounters several other reptiles that were alive during the Triassic period around the shores of Tethys. Perhaps the most unusual of these reptiles was Tanystropheus on pages 12 and 13. The long neck of this reptile was inflexible. Tanystropheus could not move its head round very easily. The Rhamphorhynchus, on page 7, were among the first pterosaurs to take to the air. Perhaps more unusual was Kuehneosaur seen on page 15. The 'wings' of this animal were, in fact, extended ribs. Though a fossil of this animal has been found near Tethys, it was much more common inland to the north-west. Placodus was a strange marine reptile that probably ate shellfish. It became extinct soon after the time of our story.

A Plesiosaurus

After millions of years the Nothosaurus line probably evolved into the Plesiosaurus, which first appeared during the Jurassic period.